W9-DJI-857

THE
Irresistible
Church SERIES

Pathways to BELONGING

Pathways to BELONGING

Creating **INCLUSIVE MINISTRY ENVIRONMENTS** for All Ages

by Debbie Lillo

Pathways to Belonging
ISBN 978-0-9965522-9-5

Author–Debbie Lillo
Contributing Authors–Kate Brueck
Collaborators–Holly Carter, Shauna Amick
Contributing Editors–Ali Howard and Mike Dobes
Editor in Chief–Marc Stein

Printed in the United States of America.

Produced by The Denzel Agency (www.denzel.org)
Cover and Interior Design: Rob Williams

For information or to order additional print copies of this and other resources contact:

Joni and Friends International Disability Center
P.O. Box 3333, Agoura Hills, California 91376-3333
Email: churchrelations@joniandfriends.org
Phone: 818-707-5664

Kindle version available at www.irresistiblechurch.org

CONTENTS

Introduction: To Fully Belong

Allow me to introduce you to a wonderful young man named Sam.[1] Sam is a kind 9-year-old boy with limited language. He is very large for his age and a challenge to re-direct. He has sensory issues but loves to engage in corporate worship. Even with one-on-one support from an assigned buddy, the children's ministry classrooms are overwhelming for Sam and he is unable to engage in the small-group setting. His mother continually worried that he would wander from the Sunday school room, so she kept him with her in the main service. To better support Sam and his mom, their church designed a hybrid program for Sam—allowing him to engage in worship, but providing a room designed especially to help kids like Sam before and after worship. This room helped Sam remain calm and created an environment in which he could learn a Sunday school lesson at his own pace. His mother was thrilled to receive this support; she now enjoys listening to the sermon uninterrupted and having the opportunity to build relationships with those around her.

We desire for our churches to be irresistible—authentic communities built on the hope of Christ that compel people affected by disability to fully belong. Sometimes our best efforts to include our friends who have disabilities fall short, and participation in Sunday morning classes is difficult for some individuals. When that happens for a child, teen, or adult with disabilities we have inadvertently made it challenging for them to learn about Jesus, and to build relationships with peers. When that individual struggles, every member of his or her family is likely affected: Without support, parents of children or teens like Sam are not able to worship fully and may find it difficult to enjoy fellowship; siblings often stay home from Sunday school and are not able to participate in the activities designed to build community; and caregivers of adults with disabilities may choose to stop attending church because their loved one struggles to participate.

Although the full-inclusion buddy model, presented in the Irresistible Church resource *Call Me Friend*, works well in many settings, we sometimes need to think beyond this model if we desire for our churches to be places of full belonging. This book is designed to give you the practical tools required to evaluate the needs of the individuals served by your ministry as you create plans that allow everyone with special needs to participate and thrive in the life of your church. Our hope is that it encourages you and makes serving these wonderful families less overwhelming. Our prayer is that in the process you find joy, and that the families you serve grow in faith as they become vital participants in the life of your church family.

Note

1. Please note that names in this book have been changed to respect the privacy of the individuals mentioned.

PART I

What Does It Mean to Fully Belong?

We must recognize that each of our friends who have disabilities is uniquely gifted and lovingly created in God's image. We will never help our friends affected by disability fully belong if we think of them as "less" and doubt God's ability to work in their lives. It is our responsibility to create a culture that welcomes these individuals and their families, that shares the gospel with them in a way that is sensitive to their learning styles and physical needs, and that helps them to discover and practice the gifts God has given them. John 14:25-26 encourages us to depend on the Holy Spirit to expand our understanding of God's words: "All this I have spoken while still with you. But the Advocate, the Holy Spirit, whom the Father will send in my name, will teach you all things and will remind you of everything I have said to you." We, therefore, need to trust that if we share the gospel with our friends with disabilities as best we know how, the Holy Spirit will fill in the gaps.

As we remove barriers and distractions, individuals of all ages who have disabilities and their families will grow in faith, their gifts will be discovered, and they will find their place in your broader church family. (Please note: within the context of this book, *buddy* is the name we have given to those who serve within special needs ministry, and *friend* is the name we have given to individuals who are served by the special needs ministry.)

Maintaining an inclusive heart, no matter how your programs are structured, demands a flexible mindset. I encourage you to embrace frequent evaluation, modifications, creativity, and spontaneity. You will find that the effort is greatly rewarded by friends who want to participate in class, maturing in faith, understanding, and practice.

University of Aberdeen theologian John Swinton says, "To belong is to be missed when you are absent." So, what does it mean for our friends who have disabilities to fully belong?

- They fully belong when they have access to every opportunity that other members of the church family enjoy.
- They fully belong when they can hear about Jesus in a way that reflects their learning style, intellectual capability, and mobility needs. This might look one way for one friend and another way for their classmate, requiring some creativity on our part.
- They fully belong when they have built quality relationships, feel at home in the church family, and are practicing their gifts for the good of the church family and the world.

We all desire to fully belong. As we begin to accommodate the unique strengths and weaknesses of individuals identified as having special needs, we also create learning, worship, and community environments that will be more welcoming to others who may struggle to belong for other reasons. And, I believe, we will often be surprised by how much our friends teach us along the way.

PART II

Determining Which Environments Will Maximize Ministry

Jamie settled in cooperatively with his designated one-on-one buddy as other children gradually arrived at Sunday school. But, as the classroom became noisy and active, he grew increasingly agitated. By the time the teacher began the lesson, Jamie was circling the classroom with his hands over his ears. His buddy used agreed-upon strategies to help calm Jamie, but his anxiety continued to mount. When another child brought a noisy toy to the teaching circle, Jamie dropped to the ground, placed his hands over his head, made loud noises, and displayed extreme anxiety. He scratched his buddy as she tried to comfort him and direct him to the sensory room.

When his parents arrived, he told them how much he hated church.

For Jamie and others like him, best efforts to thrive in a typical classroom sometimes fall short. Despite attempting to create an effective one-on-one buddy ministry, the mainstream classroom environment may not be best. Just as the school system creates an Individual Education Plan for each child, so too we need to consider each child individually, recognize that "one size does not fit all," and create a plan that allows each of our friends to hear the gospel in a way that is best suited to their learning style, sensory sensitivity, and social needs. This gospel focus is what distinguishes a church's spiritual plan from the Individual Education Plan schools design to guide special education programming for a student. The remainder of this resource will help you evaluate ministry options and will offer practical tools as you implement new strategies.

Buddy ministries are the most common approach to supporting our friends with special needs. Our Irresistible Church resource, *Call Me Friend*, will give you detailed information on setting up a buddy ministry. In short, this style of special needs ministry needs the least amount of dedicated space, and allows individuals with special needs to participate in regular classroom programming. Buddy ministries allow typically developing peers to learn side-by-side with their peers who have unique challenges. Often this kind of ministry environment creates young people who are naturally welcoming to their friends as teens and adults. Buddy ministries are the most inclusive option and are therefore ideal in many ways.

Buddy ministries are often most effective if they also include a breakout sensory option, as we will discuss shortly. They do not require a designated special needs teaching team, but they do have the potential to require a large number of designated and trained volunteers.

If you have paired a friend with one or more quality buddies and have diligently created and modified a positive behavior strategy that has fallen short, it may be time to consider whether they are in the wrong ministry environment. If an individual is not learning or building quality relationships, he may be in the wrong environment or may have the wrong support for the environment he is in. Before you decide a new environment is necessary, however, it helps to evaluate your current ministry setup and consider possible adaptations. Here are five elements of an inclusive ministry environment to consider as you evaluate your next steps:

1. *Physical Environment*: Friends who cannot fully participate will not thrive in a traditional classroom setting. Do wheelchair users have room to move and participate fully? Are you using visuals that are easily seen? Is your friend with visual or auditory limitations sitting where she can see and hear the instruction? Is the room attractive and inviting but not overwhelming for students with sensory sensitivity?
2. *Sensory Environment*: Individuals with sensory processing issues will be overwhelmed in classrooms that are filled with noises, smells, and distracting visuals. People of all kinds benefit from teaching that includes opportunities to use their senses when they learn, but the classroom environment itself might be interfering for some individuals. Do the lights flicker? Are there background noises such as the buzzing of a clock or clicking of a heater? Are the wall decorations filled with bright colors and visual distractions, or are the colors soothing and the

decorations uncluttered? Are there so many children in the class that the noise level could feel chaotic to a sensitive child?

3. *Social Environment*: Many children with disabilities struggle to interact socially. In order to learn successfully and feel comfortable in a traditional classroom, they will need an environment that intentionally nurtures relationships and models compassion. Are the teachers in your classrooms modeling acceptance? Do they welcome your buddies' efforts to help their friends with social challenges experiment with friendship development? Do the other students accept them as part of the class or do they shun them?
4. *Communication Environment*: Nonverbal friends and those with a limited ability to communicate often need information and schedules presented with picture so that they can follow along more easily. Are your classroom teachers able and willing to use visuals rather than relying solely on verbal instruction? Are nonverbal friends able to come away from learning times understanding the main point of the lesson?
5. *Cognitive Environment*: An individual's ability to learn grows exponentially when he or she is

> thoughtfully taught. With a buddy's help, many friends can learn the important nugget from regular classroom lessons. With multi-sensory teaching, most friends can participate and grow spiritually. Are there friends in your ministry who do not seem to be growing despite best efforts to creatively teach in a typical classroom?

How you respond to friends who find your classroom environment challenging will depend on the situation, but may include the following:

Disability Sensitivity Training: Setting aside time to train classroom teachers and helpers on disability awareness may go a long way towards remedying many of the barriers described above. Check out our Irresistible Church series book titled *Engaging Game Changers* for helpful training tools.

Minor Classroom Adaptations: Sometimes all that is needed for a friend to fully and successfully learn and participate are a few minor adaptations. It may be that you need to create a space in the back of the classroom filled with sensory tools. It can be a great idea to provide a buddy bag or box filled with objects particularly matched to the friend you are supporting. You may also consider restructuring group activities to allow more time in smaller, more manageable groups. Sometimes it only takes something as simple as adding a visual schedule and having teachers who will stick to a predictable schedule.

Hybrid Programs: Hybrid programs can be designed to allow your friends to spend some of their time in the regular classroom for worship, socialization and/or as the lesson is presented, but also allows for time in an environment that is better suited for learning, movement, or decompression.

Hybrid programs:

- allow friends with special needs to participate in beneficial aspects of mainstream programs;
- provide regular opportunities for friends with special needs to interact with their peers and vice versa;
- provide an evaluation season for your special needs team to decide if a self-contained classroom is warranted;
- provide friends with easy opportunities to become more fully included as they mature.

This symbol indicates that there are supplemental resources that correspond with this topic at http://www.joniandfriends.org/church-relations/

Self-Contained Classrooms: This ministry style is conducted in a room set aside for individuals who have disabilities so that they can learn at their own pace and in their own unique style, as well as interact relationally in an environment in which they are comfortable. Self-contained programs require a designated teaching team and space but can provide a quality learning environment for your friends who are not thriving in a traditional classroom or hybrid program.

Self-contained programs:

- can be personalized and easily adapted;
- allow each friend to learn in a way that meets his or her learning, sensory and mobility style;
- can be structured to allow for repetition, movement, and sensory needs;
- create an easy placement option for unexpected first-time visitors;
- provide consistency from week to week for friends who need a predictable schedule and a consistent group of people.

Before we discuss detailed guidelines for establishing these ministry models, let's take a minute to examine the relational goal of all program efforts.

PART III

Maximizing Relationships

No matter the ministry model you choose, it is important to be intentional about helping your friends and their families build quality relationships with their peers by becoming fully involved in the church family. The heart of the Irresistible Church movement is about building relationships, not programs. Well-planned programs are merely an avenue for building authentic relationships. As you move from a buddy ministry to alternative ministry environments, isolation becomes a risk, and it is especially important that you are intentionally facilitating relationships and building community. Be creative as you consider ways to encourage relationships.

The relationships you facilitate will have lasting effects on both the families and volunteers in your ministry. Over the years, I have watched God transform the hearts of many volunteers serving in disability ministry. One such volunteer is a woman named Sharon. I first met Sharon when she was 12 years old. She had a beautiful heart for the children at her school with autism. Sharon encouraged her pastor and her parents to launch a buddy program, intentionally welcoming families affected by disability on Sunday mornings. She volunteered for respite events, parent support groups, and in many other positions serving the special needs population in her community. Eventually she was asked to co-lead a growing disability ministry. Sharon is now in her third year at college and is working to become either an occupational therapist or a behavior specialist. Every individual Sharon has worked with has been blessed by her deep commitment to relationship, and it is clear that the trajectory of Sharon's life has been completely transformed and enriched by the friendships she poured into.

Please consider the following relationship-building ideas to enhance your disability ministry:

- Provide easy, one-time volunteer opportunities to help volunteers of all ages move past fears and misconceptions. Respite events and other outreach programs that support special needs families are wonderful opportunities to introduce your church members to the families you serve and set the stage for relationships to develop.

- Encourage your volunteers to pray for their friends and their families. Teach them to view the individual they serve as a friend and build a relationship with them outside of class.

- If you are not able to include all children in the regular classrooms, consider setting up *reverse inclusion*—intentionally including typically developing peers in your modified classroom settings. Friends who have special needs benefit from interaction with their peers, and the experience can be life changing for their peer mentors. As your children's teachers and youth leaders emphasize service as an outpouring of faith, they can encourage the kids in their class to consider serving through reverse-inclusion friendship.

- Discover which friends are involved in outside activities like Special Olympics, drama or soccer. Encourage your teaching team and buddies to attend one event each quarter to foster relationships.

- As you launch your new ministry plan, we encourage you to be mindful that disability affects every member of the family. You will benefit from keeping in close contact with the parents so that you are aware of what support they might need from your church family. Teachers will likely have good insight into the needs of your friends and their typical siblings. You might check to see if your church's care ministry would be willing to engage other church members to help with the ongoing care of the families supported by your ministry. When the whole family is well loved, your friend will be more likely to thrive through regular participation.

The remainder of this resource offers practical tools for creating hybrid or self-contained ministry models to support your friends and their families well. We pray that as you learn and implement the how-tos of disability ministry, life-giving friendships will ensue.

PART IV

Creating Hybrid and Self-Contained Ministries

John is a young man who attends a local church. He has intellectual disabilities, is a visual learner, and processes language slowly. As a teenager he dearly wants to participate in teen activities, although his social skills are limited. His church has begun including John in the first part of their youth program. He and two buddies join the fellowship time, enjoy the games, and participate in worship. Since John has difficulty understanding the youth teaching lesson and can be disruptive in small groups, his church has created a classroom where he and his buddies can go for the second half of the youth hour. There they enjoy a modified lesson, follow-up activities, and service projects designed especially for John and other individuals with special needs.

No matter the age of your friends, it may be time to consider a hybrid or self-contained classroom if your church experiences any of the following:

- Your friends are not thriving when paired one-on-one with a buddy and would benefit from individualized learning.
- A friend's sensory issues make it impossible for him or her to be comfortable and teachable in a large classroom setting.
- There are too many transitions or schedule changes in the regular classroom, and those teachers find it challenging to accommodate friends with disabilities by changing the class structure.
- A friend exhibits challenging behavior that could injure others. In this situation, a self-contained classroom tends to be an environment more conducive to creating and implementing a successful, positive behavior plan.

Generally, our friends who have physical limitations but typical intellectual functioning do not need the support of a self-contained classroom. However, some of these individuals have experienced socialization challenges and may want the security of a special class.

We encourage you to partner closely with parents to make the best decision for each friend in your ministry. It is wise to check with parents before moving a friend from one environment to another. Prioritize their desires whenever possible, and be sensitive if they are unwilling to disclose their child's disability or recognize their need for special accommodations. It can be a good idea to ask if their child is having similar challenges at home or school, allowing the parent to disclose information on their own terms. Once a disability is disclosed, ask the parent to complete an intake form while explaining that by receiving that information you will be able to better love and support their child within your ministry. If it is necessary to communicate a challenging situation with a parent, use the "sandwich method" by sandwiching the difficult information between positive remarks or stories about their child. This style of communicating affirms that you love their child and are committed to that child's success within your ministry.

Creating a Hybrid Ministry

It is often a good idea to create a hybrid ministry before fully launching a self-contained classroom. You may find that your friends thrive with hybrid support and do not need a fully self-contained class. Create a classroom or space designated for breakout times when a friend finds the regular classroom overwhelming. This space may be used simply as a quiet space for friends when they feel overwhelmed, but it can also be set up for instruction or lesson review. For some friends, breakout might be part of their regular classroom schedule. A hybrid space might include therapy balls, a tent, a hanging swing, beanbags, or other places your friends might go to self-regulate or calm themselves down if they have become overwhelmed in the regular classroom setting. You may also want to include Bible learning materials so that the buddy can reinforce or teach the day's lesson if needed. Check out the online appendices for this book to learn more about sensory areas and calming devices.

If your hybrid space is a dedicated classroom, it may be a less overwhelming place for buddies and friends to check in and meet for the day regardless of the classroom arrangement. Buddy bags, schedules, and intake forms can be stored in the break-out room to be available when needed.

For some individuals with sensory sensitivity, worship music is loud and overwhelming. They may need to have their own worship in a different room or outside the door with a noise-filtering headset. Some friends with this type of sensitivity might be fine to return to the classroom for teaching time.

Some churches have found that it works well to bring friends into the regular classroom for worship and social activities, but then provide a self-contained class for teaching and application time. In those cases, the secondary classroom would be set up and structured similarly to a self-contained classroom.

If you decide that your friends will receive their primary teaching in their own classroom space, you will find helpful strategies in the self-contained guidelines that follow.

Designing a Self-Contained Classroom

How you design your self-contained classroom will depend on the size and location of the room and your start-up budget. If possible, choose a room that is not isolated from the rest of the children or youth classes.

This communicates to the church body that your friends are an accepted and welcome part of the congregation. Regardless of how your church is set up, it is a good idea to allow visibility into what is happening in the room so that volunteers, leadership, and families have the opportunity to see the wonderful activities and growth taking place.

Space: Within a self-contained classroom, allow space for active lessons, dance, and re-enactment of Bible stories. Congested classrooms can cause children with sensory sensitivity to feel crowded and uncomfortable. Try to visualize how the space would work if your Bible lesson included drama, dance, or active worship.

Once you have chosen your setting, consider the needs of individuals who use wheelchairs or have other physical challenges. If the budget allows, specialty tables can be purchased that are shaped especially for wheelchair users and can be adapted to different heights. A less expensive option might be to purchase lap tables for friends who are unable to use a conventional table.

Sensory Stimulation: Consider the sensory environment. Are there lights that flicker? Are you close enough to loud external sounds that you might need sound filtering headsets? Are you close enough to outside smells that you might need to purchase toys that have a faint scent, allowing them to focus on that smell and ignore the distracting smell wafting into the classroom? As you create your room, strive to build an environment that is compelling, but not busy or overwhelming to the senses. Store your resources in tinted bins that are well marked rather than allowing friends in your class to be distracted by seeing all of the materials at once. Contrary to popular thought, gentle colors are often much more successful than bright primary colors. Providing many opportunities for sensory satisfaction without overwhelming the senses allows individuals with sensory sensitivity an environment in which they can thrive.

Setup: Some teachers have found great success setting up several stations around the room so that their friends can experience the elements of the day at their own pace. Other teachers prefer to give the same experiences one at a time. Get to know your friends and experiment with different classroom setups—it will quickly become clear what works for the friends you currently serve. But remember that what works for your friends one week might need to be modified in the future.

Icons and visuals are a useful resource for friends who are not verbal. Although you are likely to have a range of verbal and reading skills, it is probably safe to assume that you will have some friends who communicate and learn best through pictures.

Schedule: Having a schedule clearly displayed somewhere in the room is a critical component for many self-contained classrooms. Many individuals with special needs, regardless of age, feel most comfortable and in control when the schedule is predictable. This is especially true for our friends who have autism or intellectual disabilities. Choose a routine for your class and create a visual schedule that can be easily rearranged if there is a change in schedule. When you know of an irregularity in the schedule, be sure to show the revised schedule to everyone as they arrive so that they can prepare for change. Many friends who have disabilities find transitions and change challenging, and they are comforted by knowing what is coming next. In some cases, it will help to foreshadow transition by saying, "In ___ minutes we will ____." It can also be helpful to give a five-minute warning before each classroom activity change.

Safety: Consider safety issues based on the friends you plan to serve. If you have children who are prone to running away, what changes do you need to make to the classroom to minimize the chance of their escape? What are your toileting options? Do you need to secure your materials from friends who open and empty drawers and cabinets? We encourage you to check your existing church policies on liability and safety concerns. The policies in place for children and youth ministries will often mirror or overlap the policies for your ministry.

Elements of Self-Contained Classroom Learning Time

Every classroom is unique. The various elements you include will depend on how long your class will last, whether or not your friends will be spending time in the traditional classroom, your facilities, and the gifting of your teaching team. To see sample schedules for self-contained classes, check out the online appendices. When planning your classroom learning time, the following are several primary elements you will want to consider:

Learning Preparation—Consider having some sort of pre-learning activity that prepares your friends for the lesson that will be taught that day. For instance, you might fill a bean bin with objects that are part of the teaching story, or you might play a game that demonstrates the value the lesson teaches. If teaching about Noah and the ark (Genesis 6-9), for example, you might have toy animals and a boat in your teaching bin, or you might play a game that emphasizes trusting God's promises.

Worship—Most of our friends who have disabilities respond wonderfully to music. It often seems that the Holy Spirit uses music to reach their hearts in a special way. Some will even sing words they have never spoken. A time of worship can allow your friends to respond to what they have just learned about God. It builds opportunities for movement for those who find sitting still challenging. Carefully chosen songs repeat the key teaching nuggets in a way they are likely to remember. Consider creating a poster that includes picture icons for each of the songs you regularly sing. Once they become familiar with the songs, your friends could also participate in choosing a song each week. Provide your friends with simple musical instruments or ribbon wands and enjoy the beauty of unconstrained worship. For individuals who have sound sensitivities, it can be a great idea to provide noise-cancelling headphones, and do not be surprised if those friends are happiest enjoying worship from the hallway or back of the classroom.

Prayer—Prayer is simply communication with God; in light of that, never doubt that He is able to communicate with all your friends, even those who are verbally challenged. Strive to make prayer a regular element of your classroom. It can be a great idea for parents to bring in pictures of people they love so that your friends can choose whom to pray for each week. You can also regularly ask parents if there are things the class might be praying for. One nonverbal friend I know tells her parents she wants to come to church by repeating "Amen!" until they all get dressed and leave for church. Do not underestimate the power of the Holy Spirit to "intercede with sighs too deep for words" (Romans 8:26).

Teaching Time—As you plan your Bible story lesson, consider the needs of learners with special needs. Instruction should be given using realistic visuals, and it is good policy to avoid abstract concepts and phrases. Most friends who benefit from self-contained classrooms are concrete learners, and many have verbal challenges. If we want them to understand that Bible stories really happened, we should avoid cartoon characterizations that resemble make-believe.

Our illustrations ought to be clear and nuance-free, and we should avoid using metaphors, sarcasm, and Christian jargon that can be abstract. If possible, use visuals that honor and reflect the chronological age of your friends. The following are a handful of ideas to consider as you prepare your lesson:

- Friends with special needs generally learn best if they are given the opportunity to experience the teaching with their eyes, ears, bodies, and hands. Involving *all of their senses* allows them to learn more easily because they often have deficits in one learning style or another. I encourage you to spend time getting to know the learning styles of your friends and prioritize those modalities, including visuals, storytelling, and tactile learning.

- Repetition is often a great tool to help individuals with special needs learn a new concept. Consider repeating the story several ways in the course of your class, or choose a key phrase to go with each lesson and repeat that phrase regularly. Using figurines or visuals and allowing your friends to manipulate them to re-tell aspects of the story is another form of repetition. You may also consider teaching each lesson two weeks in a row, building on the teaching as you reiterate the key elements.

- Many people find it challenging to sit quietly for a full hour, especially individuals with special needs. As a solution, build movement into your teaching. For example, you could ask your friends to respond to your story with arm or body movement, or you could have them dance or march whenever your story lends itself to do so. You could also encourage them to actively create the sounds of the story. Once you begin adding movement to your lessons, you will find that the ideas are endless.

- When your friends participate in a drama, the story becomes their own. Consider keeping simple costumes and props close at hand so that drama becomes a regular occurrence.

- If your friends find language challenging, creating Yes/No cards or props to help them answer review questions can be extremely helpful.

They will appreciate having a tangible way to show you that they understand more than they are able to express in words.

- When planning your lesson, realize that every one of your friends has unique giftings and challenges. As you plan each class, consider ways to individualize your presentation for friends who might need more support. As we mentioned previously, most friends with special needs benefit from repetition, so making adaptations to the class should only help, not hurt, your friends' ability to learn.

- Flexibility is critical. Expecting that your lesson may go differently than planned is prudent. It is totally normal for something that worked well one week to go poorly the next week. Within special needs ministry, it is important to enjoy the creative process. Celebrate each element of teaching that succeeds, and trust that the Holy Spirit will fill in any gaps that you may feel were not clearly communicated or were left unsaid. It is not unusual to feel disheartened when your friends' behaviors repeatedly prevent you from conducting your planned programming. However, celebrating the little things and being intentionally grateful for the opportunity to disciple our friends produce in us a love for our friends and help eliminate frustration.

Crafts and Lesson Reinforcement—A simple, age-appropriate craft is an excellent way for your friends to bring the story home and share what they have learned. Consider your friends and your teaching team when you plan your craft; if most of your friends will need assistance, be sure that you have enough volunteers scheduled. If the majority of your friends do not enjoy crafts, consider a take-home drawing or story summary that can be decorated by those who are interested but will still tell the story for those who are not. There are a myriad of craft ideas available online. Pinterest and Google searches provide amazing ideas for nearly every Bible story or concept you might study.

Service Project—We are each created in God's image, designed with specific gifts to serve the body. We encourage you to build service into your classroom routine. Ask God to help you discern ways that each of your friends might serve your church family or community. Your friends can serve individually or as a group. If your church has a care team, you can brainstorm with them to consider service possibilities. In my community I have seen friends with disabilities serving in a variety of ways: assisting as ushers and greeters at their churches; regularly assembling church bulletins mid-week; participating in park clean-up days; making care packages for babies at a home for unwed moms; making valentines for residents at a local care facility; and caroling to residents of local group homes. Be creative as you plan—there are endless possibilities. We pray that as your church family sees your friends serving, they will begin to understand that your church is blessed because of their contributions.

Choosing and Modifying Curriculum

Every curriculum has its strengths and weaknesses. No curriculum will meet the needs of every individual in any classroom, so be prepared to adapt, no matter what you choose, and expect that the class will not go exactly as you planned. If you feel that a special needs curriculum is the best fit for your friends, we encourage you to look for curriculum that includes the elements described in the previous section, Elements of Self-Contained Classroom Learning Time, and plan to supplement elements it may be lacking. Many elements of a special needs classroom are educational practices that benefit all children; therefore, many regular curriculums can be adapted, eliminating the need to purchase curriculum designed specifically for individuals with special needs.

You may find that your church is already using a Sunday school curriculum that is easily adapted or that has elements already designed for individuals with special needs. Many disability ministries have used the preschool or primary lessons of the regular curriculum for their special needs classrooms, adding age-appropriate activities when necessary. When all age groups in the church are studying the same material, it encourages discussion and community with your friends' typically developing peers and siblings.

As you determine the curriculum for your class, consider the abilities of your friends. If your friends are intellectually high functioning but have visual, auditory, or physical disabilities, they will likely do well remaining in the regular classroom with buddy support and curriculum adaptation. If you have friends in your class who do not read or who learn better visually, consider purchasing a Bible with realistic pictures, such as *Picture That! Bible*, or *My Learn to Read Bible*.

In short, curriculum adaptation includes simplifying the content, removing abstract concepts, adding opportunities for repetition, and extracting the key nuggets of each lesson. In adapting curriculum, it is important to treat each of your friends in an age-appropriate manner. Even if a teen, adult, or older child has a significant intellectual disability and is nonverbal, they do not want to be treated like a baby or preschooler. If they learn best from children's curriculum, try to replace the illustrations to create a curriculum that respects the fact that they are older. The online appendices for this book include more detailed information on how to adapt curriculum for your special needs friends.

PART V

Special Considerations for Ministering to Various Age Groups

Each age group that you serve will have unique needs. In the following pages, we will take a look at children, teens and adults as distinct age groups within special needs ministry. Our hope is that in looking closer at each group, you will be better equipped to serve them.

Special Considerations for Ministering to Children

The guidelines given in the previous sections of this book apply to most children's ministry situations. However, when working specifically with children, it is exceptionally important that your language and concepts be concrete, that you repeat concepts in a variety of engaging ways, and that you provide a consistent schedule and routine. You will probably need to allow for more playtime when working with younger children, giving them an opportunity to burn off energy so that they can focus on the lesson. Adapting curriculum for children can be easier than other age groups because they do not feel babied by curriculum designed for children younger than themselves. As the children in your ministry age, they may begin to respond better to more mature visuals and activities. Parents of children are often still adjusting to a new diagnosis and may take special emotional care as they learn to support their child.

Special Considerations for Ministering to Teens

A local church in Northern California began a small special needs ministry by simply meeting the needs of those who came through a self-contained classroom. As they grew, the needs of their friends with special needs grew as well. The range of spiritual gifts, abilities, and needs were always changing as new friends found a home at the church. The ministry leader knew they needed to adapt if they wanted to serve all their friends well.

She asked their friends and leaders to step out of their comfort zones and created a hybrid class for Sunday mornings. She wanted their friends to worship, interact, and study the Bible with their typical peers as much as possible. Small-group leaders and buddies were trained to help friends with special needs navigate the middle and high school worship services. Some friends were able to stay in the typical youth group class with a buddy throughout the service, while others were brought back to the self-contained classroom following worship to hear the lesson in a way that matched their learning style.

One young man in particular flourished though this program. He began in the self-contained classroom and was actually the inspiration for creating the hybrid class. He now fully participates with his typical peers and even serves in the self-contained classroom once a month. The ministry leader shared this with us: "Meeting our neighbor's/friend's needs is about building and growing as the body of Christ, not about adding a program. Our goal is still to meet students where they are and love them for who God created them to be."

As we consider ministering to teens, we should remember that we fully belong when we can hear about Jesus and respond in a way that reflects our learning style, intellectual capability, and mobility needs. This might look one way for one friend and another way for their classmate, especially during the teen years when peer pressure is high and the teaching becomes more advanced than children's ministry. Take this as a wonderful opportunity to be creative! Consider reaching out to a local YoungLife Capernaum chapter. This is a gifted organization that focuses on discipleship of teens with special needs. Check out their website to find a local chapter near you: www.YoungLife.org/ForEveryKid/Capernaum.

Regardless of whether you choose to create a hybrid ministry or a self-contained classroom, consider finding ways for young adults in your congregation to become involved in the life of your friends. As teens approach adulthood, building relationships with their peers can help ease the transition into adulthood as many of these friendships will endure beyond Sunday mornings. The individuals in your ministry will likely feel more comfortable inviting their peer friends and teachers to adult activities and church events once they have built quality friendships with them. Unfortunately, many adults with special needs grow out of teen programming without lasting relationships and quickly fall away from the church. Young adult participation in teen ministry provides a wonderful prescription for avoiding that.

If a teen does not seem to be grasping the teaching lessons with the help of a one-on-one buddy, or if the youth program is too loud and unpredictable for them to feel comfortable, it may be time to consider a self-contained classroom.

You will face several unique challenges when including teens with disabilities in typical youth programming. The environmental factors that overstimulate many of our friends who are on the autistic spectrum are the very things that draw typically developing teens to youth programs. Typical youth come to youth group in part because it is loud, unpredictable, and highly social. In general, individuals on the autistic spectrum have auditory sensitivity, prefer set and predictable routines, and have social challenges. Additionally, typically developing teens are keenly aware of appearance and are sometimes quick to judge and isolate those who are different from them. Youth group is often a challenging place for any teen that does not fit in. One other challenge you may face involves youth outings. Group hangouts outside the church are generally not designed to be accessible for teens with physical challenges and are often unsafe or socially challenging for our friends with autism or intellectual disabilities. This can be overcome with intentional effort and should be considered in planning.

There are several questions you will want to ask before making a decision to launch a hybrid or self-contained youth ministry: How can you work closely with youth staff to determine which parts of the existing program might be appropriate for inclusion? Can the schedule be altered to allow more interaction? Is the leadership committed to supporting your friends even if there might be some disruption to the current youth program? Once you provide a one-on-one peer or young adult buddy for each of your friends, you can make frequent evaluations to determine what works and what is a challenge in each situation. Work closely with volunteers and leaders to emphasize inclusive attitudes by encouraging compassion and allowing them opportunities to serve children with disabilities, thereby helping them become comfortable and accepting. Consider hosting a disability sensitivity training event for your volunteers and leaders. The Irresistible Church book *Engaging Game Changers* offers several examples of training activities you might include.

A hybrid ministry is often an ideal modification for teens with special needs. This setup allows friends to participate in some portion of the youth program and feel included, while also accommodating their unique needs. There are several ways a one-on-one buddy can help friends in your ministry engage with the mainstream youth program:

- Peer buddies can help your friends mingle and socialize as they arrive. They can also help their friends navigate ice-breaker games and social events often scheduled for the beginning portion of the youth programming. Individuals with special needs may not follow all the nuances of these games, but they generally love being part of the fun atmosphere.

- Most friends with special needs enjoy joining their teen peers in worship. Having a one-on-one buddy allows them to enjoy this fellowship while still accommodating their unique needs.

- Buddies can help their friends participate in special activities and outings in which they would otherwise not be able to engage. For example, one friend in our ministry was not able to attend the youth group's all-nighter event due to the care she required at nights. One of our youth leaders offered to be her buddy for the event and drive her home when she became tired.

- Peer buddies can encourage your higher functioning friends to serve in areas of strength and interest, such as helping with worship, tech support, or setup. They can also encourage your friends by supporting them in events outside the church, such as Special Olympics or other activities your friends are engaged in.

Once you determine the unique needs of the friends in your classroom, you can determine how much time they will spend in the youth room and the self-contained classroom. Most hybrid programs offer the Bible lesson within the self-contained classroom. If you do so, please be particularly careful that your activities and visuals are not too childish, as even developmentally delayed teens tend to be very aware that they are teens and not children. If you are adapting children's curriculum for your teens, remember to revise the take-home papers and visuals to be age-appropriate. Your teenage friends want to be treated as teenagers even if their learning style is different than that of their typically developing peers. If your self-contained classroom is set up to minister to teens, create a space that any teenager would enjoy. It can also be a great idea to create opportunities for reverse inclusion–inviting typical youth into the self-contained classroom environment as peer mentors and buddies.

Special Considerations for Ministering to Adults

Allow me to share a story with you about a woman named Susie. Susie is in her 50s and is a faithful follower of Christ. She has a speech impediment because of a childhood cleft palate and also has slight learning disabilities. She heard that a community church was offering a class for adults with disabilities, so she decided to take time away from her home church to check it out. She arrived at the class and found adults with disabilities sitting around a table set up in a children's ministry room. They were given children's coloring pages, sang "Jesus Loves Me," and were given juice and graham crackers for snack. Susie was insulted to be treated like a child simply because she has a disability, and she never returned to the class.

Because adult education classes are typically elective, the process of creating learning and fellowship opportunities for adults with disabilities looks very different than it does for children and youth. Ideally, for adult friends who have grown up in the church, friendships that have been developed in a teen ministry can carry over into young adult years. Because adult Sunday school is often run more independently than children or teen ministry, you will want to consider setting up a point person your friends and their families can approach with questions. This will greatly minimize confusion and miscommunication and will offer great comfort to the families. This person can also help encourage the group to find ways of integrating with the rest of the church family.

When planning an adult ministry, it is helpful to consider the greatest need of the adults you wish to serve. Most adults desire the following:

- Fellowship with similar adults
- Finding a place of belonging in the church as a whole

- Hearing the gospel presented in a manner they can understand
- Knowing how to make and keep friends at church
- Access to activities that currently present physical barriers
- Opportunities to serve and to be celebrated for their unique gifting

The needs of the adults in your class may vary widely. Consider the intellectual functioning of the adults you wish to serve as intellectual capabilities will greatly guide classroom decisions. We have identified four common groups of adults within disability ministry:

- *Adults with physical disabilities but typical intellectual function.* If the adults you serve have physical disabilities but typical intellectual function, allow them to speak into your decisions. Typically, these individuals are seeking fellowship and Bible study in accessible environments. They want their needs to be considered when outings are planned, and they want full access to the programs offered to the typical adults of your church. Sometimes these adults are seeking fellowship and support from a group of other believers who share their physical struggles. Often these individuals do not require special programming; they simply need intentional access to existing programs.

- *Adults with average or above average intelligence but social challenges.* Some adults have average or above average intelligence but struggle with social challenges. These individuals would benefit greatly from a ministry model that intentionally equips peer mentors who will faithfully show up and encourage conversation. In doing so, they will initiate safe opportunities for their friend to gradually become comfortable and skilled in building friendships with other adults in the church.

- *Adults with intellectual disabilities.* Adults with intellectual disabilities will often thrive in self-contained ministry models similar to those we have discussed for children and teens but may require age-appropriate adjustments. It is important for these adults to be given adequate opportunities to be included in fellowship activities with the typical adults of the church. Adults with high functioning autism or slight intellectual disabilities might enjoy being drawn into a leadership role within the class, such as helping to organize projects or being the technology assistant.

Self-contained or hybrid ministries for adults with intellectual disabilities, whether they take place on Sunday mornings or weeknights, should have a heavy emphasis on community building. Within that context, your friends can benefit from all the ministry components described throughout this book, including lively worship, Bible lessons, food, fun and fellowship. The leader of this class should freely present the gospel, trusting that the Holy Spirit will fill in the gaps as they are faithful to present it in ways that accommodate the physical, intellectual and sensory needs of the class members.

As we mentioned with teens, it is important to create a classroom that adults, with and without disability, would enjoy spending time in, avoiding the use of childish pictures and decorations. Classrooms should be set up to accommodate physical and sensory needs. Within the context of your ministry and within the church as a whole, help your friends recognize their gifts and find opportunities to serve. Each of your friends is marvelously and intentionally created with gifts and talents to share.

To spread your ministry beyond the individuals who attend, consider bringing in church members to share about their interesting hobbies or jobs. This will not only inspire your friends to evaluate their professional interests, but it also has the potential to initiate mentor opportunities when your friends are interested in the hobby or job that was shared. You may also consider teaching life skills such as planning meals, understanding public transportation, and handling money. The possibilities are endless and your friends will be much faster to learn those skills within the safe and trusted environment you have created.

The friends in your ministry may also appreciate having a buddy who will sit with them during the main worship service, shifting the focus to more of a hybrid ministry. Consider offering training opportunities that equip your church to welcome your friends into corporate worship with sensitivity and enthusiasm. As you build your ministry, we pray that your worship leaders and pastoral staff are encouraged to celebrate unique worship and learning styles. Our Irresistible Church series book *Enter In* provides many helpful insights and tools for inclusive worship.

CONCLUSION

Finding Joy in the Inclusion Process

Lucy loves to sing, especially songs about her Sunday school Bible lesson. She also loves participating in classroom dramas that help her learn. Lucy participates in a hybrid program while her mother enjoys attending the worship service and hearing the sermon. When the hybrid program began at their church, Lucy's mom was curious to see how it would work. Within a few weeks of joining the class, it became clear that Lucy was using words more frequently and remembering details more clearly at Sunday school than in her school classroom. Her mother began to stay after class to hear Lucy sing songs or shout out memory verses. As Lucy learned key biblical principals, her mother grew in her understanding as well. She marveled at how much her daughter was capable of learning, and even brought someone from the school to see how well Lucy learns when the classroom is structured for her success. As Lucy and her mother began to thrive, the classroom teachers were greatly encouraged to see God using their efforts to effect great change.

Our hope is that you find true joy as you walk the path to unlocking what makes each of your friends thrive. Discovering their ideal learning style, social environment, and sensory sensitivities can often transform the entire family. Once the barriers to belonging have been removed, your friends can learn about Jesus, build relationships with peers, and discover their gifts.

We recognize that adapting existing ministry models can be challenging and sometimes discouraging. We pray that you will not lose sight of the bigger picture—that you not forget that your hard work will enable friends of all ages to hear the most wonderful story ever told, the gospel. As the Apostle Paul exhorted us, "be steadfast, immovable, always abounding in the work of the Lord, knowing that in the Lord your labor is not in vain" (1 Corinthians 15:58). If we prayerfully strive to create an environment for ministry and relationship building, the Holy Spirit fills in the gaps and weaves our beloved friends and their families into the fabric of our churches. That wonderful tapestry is irresistible to the watching world and makes the body of Christ truly compelling.

Becoming *Irresistible*

Luke 14 commands Christ followers to "Go quickly . . . find the blind, the lame, and the crippled . . . and compel them to come in!" While this sounds inspiring and daunting, exciting and overwhelming, motivating and frightening, all at the same time, what does it actually mean? How do we live and function within the church in such a way that families affected by disability are compelled to walk through our doors to experience the body of Christ?

We can certainly *compel* them by offering programs, ministries, events, and other church activities, but what if the compelling aspect was more about heart, culture, acceptance and embracing? What if our churches were overflowing with the hope of Jesus Christ . . . a hope not simply for those who "fit in" or look the part, but rather a hope to all, including the marginalized, downtrodden and outcast?

Becoming *Irresistible* is more than programs and activities–it is about a transformational work in our hearts . . . first as individuals and then as the body of Christ. *Irresistible* allows us to see each individual as he or she truly is: created in the image of God (Genesis 1:26-27), designed purposely as a masterpiece (Psalm 139:13-14), instilled with purpose, plans and dreams (Jeremiah 29:11), and a truly indispensable member of the kingdom of God (1 Corinthians 12:23). An *Irresistible Church* is an "authentic community built on the hope of Christ that compels people affected by disability to fully belong." It is powerful for a person to know that he or she is fully welcomed and belongs. *Irresistible* captures the heart of the church as it should be—how else do we explain the rapid growth and intense attraction to the church in the book of Acts? The heart of God was embodied through the people of God by the Spirit of God . . . and that is simply *Irresistible*!

The Irresistible Church Series is designed to help not only shape and transform the heart of the church, but also to provide the practical steps and activities to put *flesh* around the *heart* of the church—to help your church become a place for people to fully belong. Thank you for responding to the call to become *Irresistible*. It will not happen overnight, but it will happen. As with all good things, it requires patience and perseverance, determination and dedication, and ultimately an underlying trust in the faithfulness of God. May God bless you on this journey. Be assured that you are not alone—there are many on the path of *Irresistible*.

For more information or to join the community,
please visit www.irresistiblechurch.org.

Joni and Friends was established in 1979 by Joni Eareckson Tada, who at 17 was injured in a diving accident, leaving her a quadriplegic. Since its inception, Joni and Friends has been dedicated to extending the love and message of Christ to people who are affected by disability whether it is the disabled person, a family member, or friend. Our objective is to meet the physical, emotional, and spiritual needs of this group of people in practical ways.

Joni and Friends is committed to recruiting, training, and motivating new generations of people with disabilities to become leaders in their churches and communities. Today, the Joni and Friends International Disability Center serves as the administrative hub for an array of programs which provide outreach to thousands of families affected by disability around the globe. These include two radio programs, an award-winning television series, the Wheels for the World international wheelchair distribution ministry, Family Retreats which provide respite for those with disabilities and their families, Field Services to provide church training along with educational and inspirational resources at a local level, and the Christian Institute on Disability to establish a firm biblical worldview on disability-related issues.

From local neighborhoods to the far reaches of the world, Joni and Friends is striving to demonstrate to people affected by disability, in tangible ways, that God has not abandoned them–he is with them–providing love, hope, and eternal salvation.

Available Now in the Irresistible Church Series

Start with Hello

Introducing Your Church to Special Needs Ministry

Families with special needs often share that they desire two things in their church: accessibility and acceptance. Accessibility to existing structures, programs and people is an imperative. Acceptance with a sense of belonging by the others who also participate in the structures, programs and fellowship of the church is equally necessary. In this simple book you'll learn the five steps to becoming an accessible and accepting church.

To receive first notice of upcoming resources, including respite, inclusive worship and support groups, please contact us at churchrelations@joniandfriends.org.

Available Now in the Irresistible Church Series

Call Me Friend

Building Compelling Relationships Through One-on-One Ministry

For the ministry leader who desires to include people of all ages with special needs in the life of the church, this practical guide to buddy ministry provides clear, concise direction on how to organize and implement this effective ministry model. Leaders will discover how buddies provide discipleship, friendship, safety, participation, communication and positive behavior management. The simple steps you'll find in this book will build relationships and assist your church in becoming an authentic community where all people may fully belong.

To receive first notice of upcoming resources, including respite, inclusive worship and support groups, please contact us at churchrelations@joniandfriends.org.

Other Recommended Resources

Beyond Suffering Bible

The *Beyond Suffering Bible* by Joni and Friends is the first study Bible made specifically for those who suffer and the people who love them. Uplifting insights from Joni Eareckson Tada and numerous experts and scholars who have experienced suffering in their own lives and will help you move beyond the "why" of suffering to grasp the eternal value God is building into our lives. Special features include: inspiring devotionals, biblical and contemporary profiles, Bible reading plans, connection points and disability ministry resources.

Find out more at http://www.joniandfriends.org/store/category/bibles/

Beyond Suffering® Student Edition

Beyond Suffering for the Next Generation: A Christian View on Disability Ministry will equip young people to consider the issues that affect people with disabilities and their families, and inspire them to action. Students who embrace this study will gain confidence to join a growing, worldwide movement that God is orchestrating to fulfill Luke 14:21-23: "Go out quickly into the streets and alleys of the town and bring in the poor, the crippled, the blind, and the lame.... so that my house will be full."

ISBN: 978-0-9838484-6-2
304 pages · 8.5" x 11"
Includes CD-ROM

Joni: An Unforgettable Story

In this unforgettable autobiography, Joni reveals each step of her struggle to accept her disability and discover the meaning of her life. The hard-earned truths she discovers and the special ways God reveals his love are testimonies to faith's triumph over hardship and suffering. This new edition includes an afterword, in which Joni talks about the events that have occurred in her life since the book's original publication in 1976, including her marriage and the expansion of her worldwide ministry to families affected by disability.

ISBN: 978-0310240013
205 pages · Paperback

www.joniandfriends.org · P.O. Box 3333, Agoura Hills, CA 91376
(818) 707-5664 · Fax: (818) 707-2391 TTY: (818) 707-9707

Customizable Resources from the Book

Available for Download at

http://www.joniandfriends.org/church-relations/

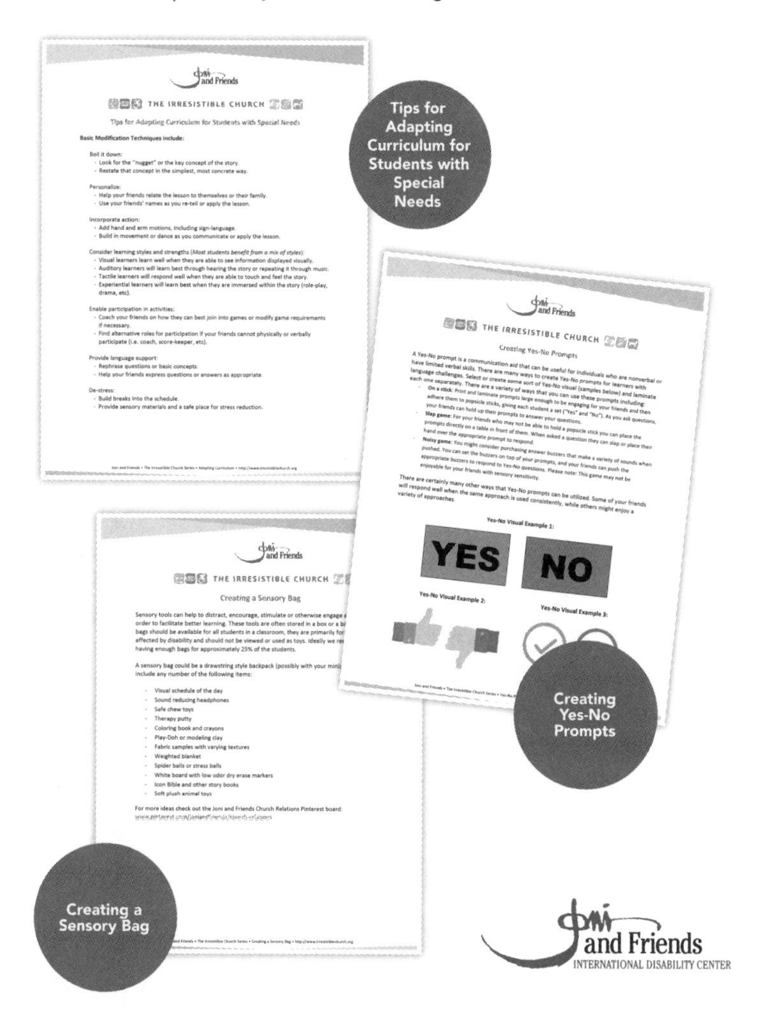

Joni and Friends

THE IRRESISTIBLE CHURCH

Tips for Adapting Curriculum for Students with Special Needs

Basic Modification Techniques include:

Boil it down:
- Look for the "nugget" or the key concept of the story.
- Restate that concept in the simplest, most concrete way.

Personalize:
- Help your friends relate the lesson to themselves or their family.
- Use your friends' names as you re-tell or apply the lesson.

Incorporate action:
- Add hand and arm motions, including sign-language.
- Build in movement or dance as you communicate or apply the lesson.

Consider learning styles and strengths (*Most students benefit from a mix of styles*):
- Visual learners learn well when they are able to see information displayed visually.
- Auditory learners will learn best through hearing the story or repeating it through music.
- Tactile learners will respond well when they are able to touch and feel the story.
- Experiential learners will learn best when they are immersed within the story (role-play, drama, etc).

Enable participation in activities:
- Coach your friends on how they can best join into games or modify game requirements if necessary.
- Find alternative roles for participation if your friends cannot physically or verbally participate (i.e. coach, score-keeper, etc).

Provide language support:
- Rephrase questions or basic concepts.
- Help your friends express questions or answers as appropriate.

De-stress:
- Build breaks into the schedule.
- Provide sensory materials and a safe place for stress reduction.

Joni and Friends • The Irresistible Church Series • Adapting Curriculum • http://www.irresistiblechurch.org

Joni and Friends

THE IRRESISTIBLE CHURCH

Creating Yes-No Prompts

A Yes-No prompt is a communication aid that can be useful for individuals who are nonverbal or have limited verbal skills. There are many ways to create Yes-No prompts for learners with language challenges. Select or create some sort of Yes-No visual (samples below) and laminate each one separately. There are a variety of ways that you can use these prompts including:
- **On a stick:** Print and laminate prompts large enough to be engaging for your friends and then adhere them to popsicle sticks, giving each student a set ("Yes" and "No"). As you ask questions, your friends can hold up their prompts to answer your questions.
- **Slap game:** For your friends who may not be able to hold a popsicle stick you can place the prompts directly on a table in front of them. When asked a question they can slap or place their hand over the appropriate prompt to respond.
- **Noisy game:** You might consider purchasing answer buzzers that make a variety of sounds when pushed. You can set the buzzers on top of your prompts, and your friends can push the appropriate buzzers to respond to Yes-No questions. Please note: This game may not be enjoyable for your friends with sensory sensitivity.

There are certainly many other ways that Yes-No prompts can be utilized. Some of your friends will respond well when the same approach is used consistently, while others might enjoy a variety of approaches.

Yes-No Visual Example 1:

YES NO

Yes-No Visual Example 2:

Yes-No Visual Example 3:

Joni and Friends • The Irresistible Church Series • Yes-No P

Joni and Friends

THE IRRESISTIBLE CHURCH

Creating a Sensory Bag

Sensory tools can help to distract, encourage, stimulate or otherwise engage order to facilitate better learning. These tools are often stored in a box or a b bags should be available for all students in a classroom, they are primarily for affected by disability and should not be viewed or used as toys. Ideally we re having enough bags for approximately 25% of the students.

A sensory bag could be a drawstring style backpack (possibly with your mini include any number of the following items:

- Visual schedule of the day
- Sound reducing headphones
- Safe chew toys
- Therapy putty
- Coloring book and crayons
- Play-Doh or modeling clay
- Fabric samples with varying textures
- Weighted blanket
- Spider balls or stress balls
- White board with low odor dry erase markers
- Icon Bible and other story books
- Soft plush animal toys

For more ideas check out the Joni and Friends Church Relations Pinterest board: www.pinterest.com/joniandfriends/church-relations

Joni and Friends • The Irresistible Church Series • Creating a Sensory Bag • http://www.irresistiblechurch.org